WITHDRAWN

glitter!

A Celebration of Sparkle

ADAMS MEDIA

NEW YORK   LONDON   TORONTO   SYDNEY   NEW DELHI

Adams media

Adams Media
An Imprint of Simon & Schuster, Inc.
57 Littlefield Street
Avon, Massachusetts 02322

First Adams Media hardcover edition October 2018

ADAMS MEDIA and colophon are trademarks of Simon & Schuster.

For information about special discounts for bulk purchases, please contact Simon & Schuster Special Sales at 1-866-506-1949 or business@simonandschuster.com.

The Simon & Schuster Speakers Bureau can bring authors to your live event. For more information or to book an event contact the Simon & Schuster Speakers Bureau at 1-866-248-3049 or visit our website at www.simonspeakers.com.

Interior design by Colleen Cunningham
Image credits listed at the end of this book

Manufactured in China

10 9 8 7 6 5 4 3 2 1

Library of Congress Cataloging-in-Publication Data
Adams Media (firm), author.
Glitter! / Adams Media.
Avon, Massachusetts: Adams Media, 2018.
LCCN 2018011467 | ISBN 9781507208212 (hc) | ISBN 9781507208229 (ebook)
Subjects: LCSH: Glitter art--Juvenile literature.
Classification: LCC TT880 .G56 2018 | DDC 745.59--dc23
LC record available at https://lccn.loc.gov/2018011467

ISBN 978-1-5072-0821-2
ISBN 978-1-5072-0822-9 (ebook)

Introduction

Glitter in your heart? Sparkles on the brain? Tell me about it, sister! There is hardly an accessory—or should I say lifestyle?—as beloved worldwide as our dazzling friend glitter. And what *couldn't* use a little sparkle? Answer: nothing. From dazzling eyeshadows and shimmering skin to glistening stemware and sparkling slippers, nothing gives your skin, wardrobe, or home more glitz and glamour than glitter. We understand your love of all that glitters, and that's why we've created *Glitter!*, the only companion you will ever need for living a life that truly sparkles.

So if you're looking for a celebration of all things glitter, you're in the right place! This book is packed with interesting facts and tips for getting the most out of your shimmer-ventures; easy glitter crafts; and inspiring quotes that will empower you to carpe the sparkle out of every diem.

How long has glitter been around? And why *are* we so crazy about it? In *Glitter!* you'll learn just how long ago the first glamoristas released their inner sparkle (hint: think caves!), and what makes us so easily distracted by all things shiny. Page upon page is gorgeously illustrated with—you guessed it—glitter! And perforated pages let you tear out and display some of our favorite glitterfied quotes, so you can bedazzle even the drabbest spaces. You will find quick and easy DIYs for everything from fabulous glitzy nail polish to glistening red heels that would make even the Wicked Witch of the West envious. There's no place like a home filled with sparkle!

But before you get into the nitty-glittery of the book, check out our chapter on the basics of glitter. What is it made of, anyway? The answer is a bit more detailed than you might think! Earth-friendly to skin-friendly, sophisticated gold to neon pink—there's a glitter out there for everything. But no need to be overwhelmed: we've got you covered! With *Glitter!* you will find everything you need to know to release your inner sparkle—because you can never have too much shine.

Glitter! What is it good for? Everything!

You are champing at the bit, ready to release your inner sparkle—but hold on a minute! There are a few things you should know before getting started.

Metallic. Pearlescent. Iridescent— Oh My!

You're asking, "Isn't all glitter the same?" No! Glitter comes in all sorts of shapes, sizes, and materials, so you can add sparkle to anything—or, let's be honest, *everything*. The main types of glitter are craft, eco-friendly, edible, and cosmetic:

Craft

Craft glitter is great for DIY projects and activities where you don't need to worry about ingesting the particles. There are tons of craft glitters out there, but the key types are:

Standard polyester: the most common material that glitter is made from. The itty-bitty pieces cut from polyester (a.k.a. glitter) can be either translucent (see-through shades of color) or opaque (solid bright colors and reflective metallics).

Hologram: an edgy glitter that is made with a metallic finish that gives it the unique sparkle of a dozen colors wrapped into one.

Solvent resistant: a heavy-duty polyester (for the truly die-hard DIYers out there) that can withstand most solvents and extreme heat without the colors bleeding out. *Bye-bye,* streaky nail polish.

Diamond Dust: the name alone is *très chic.* Known as the glitteriest of all glitters, Diamond Dust gets its eye-grabbing shine from the tiny flakes of glass that it is made from. When caught in the light, these flakes reflect a uniquely dazzling sparkle—just like diamonds! So really, *glitter* is a girl's best friend.

So crack open your Mod Podge, crafters, because your next project is sure to dazzle!

Eco-Friendly

This glitter is made from natural ingredients like vegetables, seaweed, minerals, and other biodegradable materials that will make you feel good about saving the planet! This special glitter is perfect for all the glamourous glitter fiends out there who want to keep on shining while still being kind to Mother Earth. Sparkle on, "green" goddesses!

Edible

Did you know you can have your...glitter, and *eat* it too? Edible glitter is commonly made from a mixture of sugar, gum arabic, and cornstarch, and is a popular accessory in baking. Dazzle guests with cupcakes topped with shimmering edible pearls, and cakes that glisten to make a queen swoon. Eating *can* be glamorous.

Cosmetic

Cosmetic-grade glitter is made from a nontoxic (no angry red blemishes!) polyester that uses pigment rather than dye to keep colors from bleeding out and staining. What's that sound? A chorus of eager fashionistas all asking what professional gave you that fabulous shimmering cat-eye. Popular cosmetic glitters are Mylar flakes (thin, translucent pieces of glitter that sparkle like crystals) and pearlescent glitter (ultrafine particles that gleam just like a lustrous pearl!!). Rock those sparkles from head to toe and shine on, worry-free!

Glitter All Day, Every Day!

Craft, edible, cosmetic: there is *always* room for glitter. And just like everything is better with glitter, glitter is better when used correctly. A few things to keep in mind to make the most of your glitter experiences:

Always **read packaging labels:** Though a label may say "food safe," it does not necessarily mean that the glitter is edible. Always make sure the label specifically says "edible" before using the product in food preparation. Labels will also tell you if a glitter is highly flammable and needs to be handled with a bit more care.

Use glitter for its intended purpose: Cosmetic glitter for skin, edible glitter for food, and craft glitter for your DIY projects. Even if you take pride in having an iron stomach, *play it safe*.

And now that you're an expert on all that sparkles, it's finally time to move on to the *really* shiny part (you may need sunglasses). Ready, set, glitter!

WONDERING HOW  GOT ITS NAME?

IT WASN'T FROM ACCIDENTAL INVENTOR HENRY RUSCHMANN! THE MODERN WORD *GLITTER* COMES FROM THE MIDDLE ENGLISH WORD *GLITEREN,* WHICH ITSELF WAS ADAPTED FROM THE OLD NORSE WORD *GLITRA.* BOTH TRADITIONAL WORDS TRANSLATE TO *TO GLISTEN.* OUR ANCESTORS KNEW—ALL THAT GLITTERS IS GORGEOUS.

She who
leaves a trail
of glitter
is never
forgotten.

Dreaming of a sparkly new year?

Make your own magical glitter snow globe
in just a few easy steps!

All you need is:

Superglue
Plastic decoration
Glass jar with lid
Glitter

Next:

1. Glue your decoration to the inside of the jar lid.

2. Fill the jar with water and craft glitter.

3. Glue the inner rim of the lid and twist tightly onto the jar.

4. Once the glue has dried, flip the jar upside down and *ta-da*: it's snowing glitter!

Glitter isn't just for the modern fashionista.

People were sewing sparkle into their clothing as early as the 1400s, when shiny metals were used to accent tunics and dresses. No need to hit the gym when you're carrying pounds of pewter on your outfit!

She's bright like glitter and bubbly like champagne.

DON'T BE AFRAID TO SPARKLE.

DON'T LET ANYONE EVER DULL YOUR SPARKLE.

LIGHTS, CAMERA, GLITTER!

All you need to get the perfect glamour shot is some glitter and your phone:

1. Gather a handful of glitter in your open palms and have a friend stand a few feet in front of you with a camera phone.

2. Now one...two...three...*blow*! Send sparkling glitter swirls toward your friend while she snaps a picture—or three.

We use how much ?!

Between 1989 and 2009,
more than **10 million pounds**
of glitter was purchased in the US.
But really though, can you ever
have too much glitter?

EAT GLITTER FOR BREAKFAST AND SHINE ALL DAY

And when all the glitter
fades there'll still be stardust
in her veins.

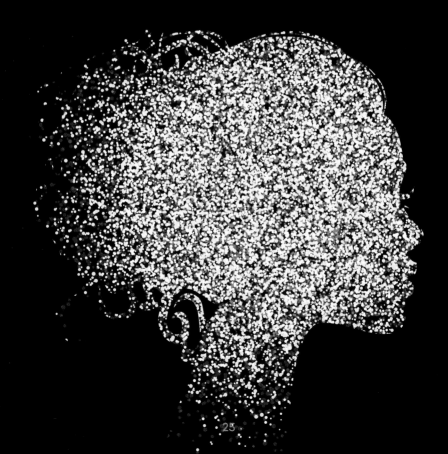

GLITTER IS A FORENSIC TREASURE THAT LAW ENFORCEMENT HAS USED TO CRACK CASES ON MULTIPLE OCCASIONS. IN 2001, INVESTIGATORS IN MISSOURI USED GLITTER TO CONNECT A SUSPECT TO THE CRIME SCENE. SHIMMERING SWINDLERS BEWARE!

BUSTED!

Home decor
in need of a little
oomph?

Turn your boring candles into classy
accents with a little tape, a paintbrush,
Mod Podge, and glitter:

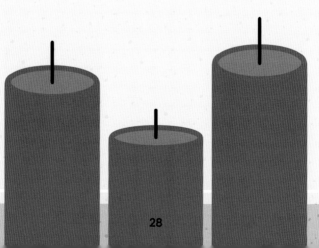

1. Tape off sections of the candle where you want your glitter to go.

2. Use a brush to apply a coat of Mod Podge to the candle.

3. Pour your glitter over the candle, turning it to ensure you get every side.

4. Peel off the tape, and *voilà*! We want to hang out at *your* house.

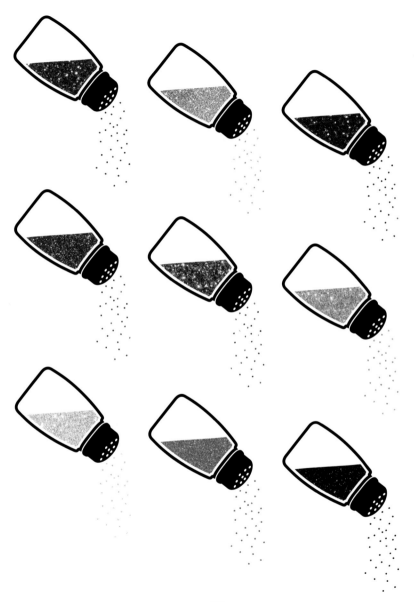

Glitter-fy like a pro: use clear salt-and-pepper shakers to organize glitter and apply to your projects without the mess. No glitter novices *here*!

SKIP THE STICKY CONDIMENTS:

MUSICIAN IGGY POP USED TO

COAT HIS BODY WITH PEANUT

BUTTER ON STAGE BEFORE

DISCOVERING GLITTER WAS

A MORE GLAMOROUS,

ALBEIT LESS SCRUMPTIOUS,

FASHION STATEMENT.

When life gives you Monday, dip it in *glitter* and *sparkle* all day.

AHHHHH, GLITTER SPILL!

Use a lint roller to
pick up runaway
glitter with ease.

THERE IS NO
SUCH THING
AS ENOUGH
GLITTER

Life is better when you are covered in glitter.

You're *covered* in glitter—it's a dream come true! But now it's time to say ta-ta 'til next time. No problem, just follow these steps for easy glitter removal:

1. Dab body glitter with sticky tape.

2. Wash your skin with an oil cleanser, then rinse off with water.

Sparkles for Santa

In 2011,
Toronto, Canada, used
over 150 *pounds* of glitter
for its Santa Claus Parade.
Talk about a *sparktacular*
introduction.

Did you know there's science behind our love for all things shiny?

It's true! Our need for H_2O keeps us on the lookout for shimmering rivers and streams, resulting in a preference for things that sparkle. So really, you had no choice *but* to buy that glittery top...

Add a touch

of shiny charm

to any room

in need of

some flair with

glitter magnets!

First, gather:

Superglue
Paintbrush
Clear flat-back marbles
Glitter
Varnish
Magnets

Then...

1. Dab glue on the flat back of the marble and spread with the paintbrush.

2. Dip the marble in glitter.

3. Apply varnish over the glitter, then let dry.

4. Glue the magnet to the flat back of the marble.

When in doubt, just add glitter

If you don't own anything glittery,

you're living life all wrong.

'Tis the season to sparkle.

Glam up an everyday hairstyle in seconds by adding fine **glitter** to a bottle with hair spray. Mist braids, roots, or hair tips for tresses that **dazzle!**

Sparkle on, darling

You were born to sparkle

Fabulous... firepower?

During World War II, the US Air Force used a strategy that consisted of releasing chaff— aluminum glitter—from the back of warplanes to confuse enemy radar.

Make a (*dishwasher-safe*) glitter-dipped mug with these easy-to-find items:

Masking tape
Glass or porcelain mug
Paintbrush
Dishwasher-safe Mod Podge
Glitter

1. Tape off your mug, and use the paint-brush to apply Mod Podge below the tape line.

2. Now go glitter-crazy!

3. Peel off tape and let dry for 4–8 hours.

4. Use paintbrush to dab a coat of Mod Podge over the glitter. Let sit for 28 days before washing. Beware: friends will be tempted to "borrow" it.

SIP YOUR
FAVORITE
BEVERAGE
IN STYLE

The first tailored
suits for women shone:
the outfits were accented
with metallic details like
threads woven with silver.
No dull duds for these
trendsetters.

Pour some Glitter on me.

From milk baths to insect facials, **Cleopatra** knew there were no limits to achieving beauty. She used crushed *beetles* (yes, the bug!) to give her skin and clothing a shimmer to match her **glamorous personality.**

KEEP CALM AND GLITTER ON

What's more versatile than Mason jars? Nothing! So why not make them a little more glamorous? All you need is a little tape, Mod Podge, and glitter:

1. Tape off sections of your jar that you want glitter-free (if *any*).

2. Apply Mod Podge.

3. Get sparkling!

4. Let jar dry before filling with... almost anything! Maybe even more glitter...

You mustn't

be afraid to

sparkle

a little brighter.

THERE IS A
TIME AND PLACE
FOR GLITTER:
ALWAYS AND
EVERYWHERE!

Gloomy day got you down?

Coat a plain pair of rain boots with glitter spray paint and bring sunshine with you wherever you go!

Get the shimmering skin
of your dreams in *minutes*:
just mix body oil with
cosmetic-grade glitter
and apply to your skin.

Bring it on, bathing suit season!

I DON'T SWEAT,

I sparkle.

A little glitter never hurt.

What is your glitter personality?

Take this quick quiz to find out!

1. **During a night on the town you wear:**
   A. Long black gown and simple gold studs
   B. Hot pink jumper with animal print clutch
   C. Deep blue wrap dress
   D. Studded black leather jacket with silver skirt

2. **Your favorite pair of kicks are:**
   A. Small black heels that go with everything
   B. Strappy yellow sandals
   C. Converse high tops
   D. Studded boots

3. **Spirit animal?:**
   A. Cat
   B. Unicorn
   C. Octopus
   D. Iguana

You are:

mostly As

Gilded Goddess: Class only *begins* to describe you. You ooze a sophistication that others aspire to. Your glitter accessory: glistening gold eyeliner.

mostly Bs

Rainbow Romantic: You see things through the lens of vivid Technicolor. The world is your oyster and you are more than ready to explore it—with a fabulous sense of style to boot! Your glitter accessory: rainbow glitter nail polish.

mostly Cs

Mystical Mermaid: The depths of mystery are where you belong. You are the gorgeous enigma that people want to know—and dress like! Your glitter accessory: teal lip shimmer.

mostly Ds

Metallic Maverick: Did someone say rebel? You go against the grain in every part of life, and you do it with an edgy glamour that leaves people enchanted. Your glitter accessory: metallic eyeshadow.

Cherish
the Way You
Sparkle

GLITTER for PRESIDENT:

In 2011, gay rights activist Nick Espinosa used the first "glitter bomb"
to shower presidential candidate Newt Gingrich with multicolored sparkles.
As they rained down on Gingrich, Espinosa exclaimed: "Feel the rainbow,
Newt!" He definitely *saw* the rainbow for a while afterward!

DON'T RAIN ON MY PARADE
JUST BECAUSE YOURS DOESN'T
HAVE ENOUGH GLITTER.

KEEP GLITTER IN ALL THE *RIGHT* PLACES BY USING AN OUTER COAT OF MOD PODGE TO SEAL YOUR DIYS.

UNLEASH

YOUR INNER

SPARKLE

SPARKLE
EVERY DAY

No one will forget to use *these* fabulously sparkly drink coasters. Just grab:

Paintbrush
Mod Podge
Round cork coasters
Glitter

Coat one side of the coasters with Mod Podge using the paintbrush, then cover in glitter and let dry.

For an even more classy take, use two colors—separating them on each side of the coaster surface, with a blend of the two in the center.

During the pivotally glamorous 1920s, women were sewing shiny beads and sequins into their clothing—

so much so, in fact, that the dresses were weighing them down. Talk about "heavy metal!"

Do more of what
makes you sparkle

No need to worry about matching
sparkle styles with a friend:

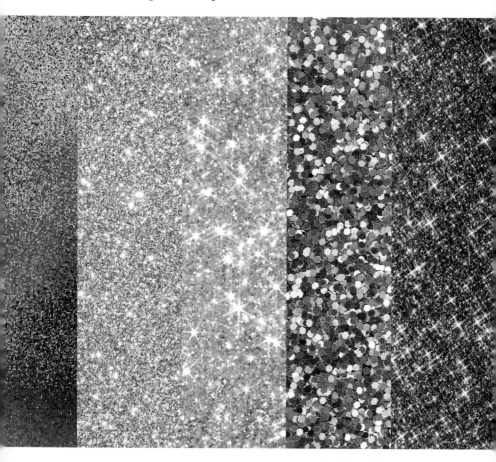

There are more than 20,000 unique types
of glitter on the market.

superb,
dazzling,
darling

Body by Glitter:

Celebs and Internet stars have daringly highlighted their body "flaws" with glitter, owning the imperfections that make them so perfectly unique. Now it's *your* turn to shine, so grab your camera, lustrous lady, and flaunt what you've got with a little extra sparkle!

Ever heard the saying, "*Accidents* happen for a reason"? It's true, and here's proof.

Glitter as we know it today was invented *accidentally* in the 1930s by a machinist named Henry Ruschmann. He was trying to create a way to dispose of waste by *crushing* plastic.

The outcome was a bit... *brighter* than he imagined.

SCHEMING BUSINESS OWNER MARGARET MARTIN WAS FINED OVER £13,000 IN 2014, AFTER SHE SOLD QUITE INEDIBLE "EDIBLE GLITTER" UNDER THE NAME EDABLE ART LTD.

SHE LATER CLAIMED THE NAME WAS ACTUALLY REFERRING TO THREE MICE NAMED ED, ABLE, AND ART.

NICE TRY, MARG. (NOT!)

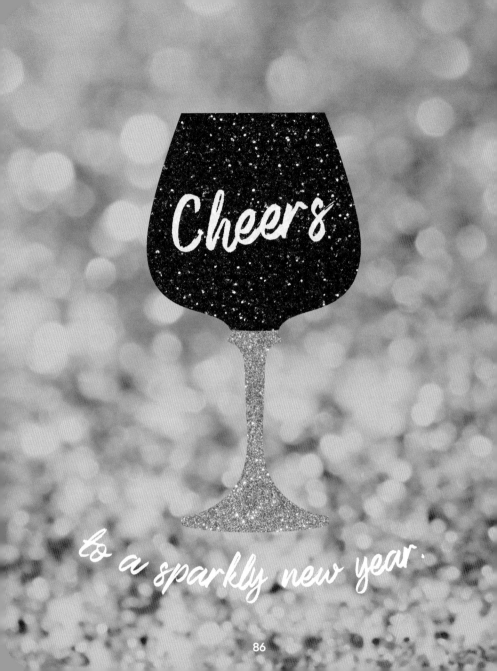

Cheers

to a sparkly new year.

Make a toast that *twinkles*! Follow our easy instructions for elegant sparkling juice glasses: all you will need are stemmed wine glasses, Mod Podge, and glitter!

1. Coat the base and stem of the wine glass with Mod Podge.

2. Apply your glitter, twisting the glass to get every angle evenly, then let dry.

3. Add a bit of sparkling grape juice and toast to a glittering year.

spread
the
sparkle

SHE BLEEDS GLITTER

WHAT DO THIS BOOK AND CAVEMEN HAVE IN COMMON?

Glitter! No, *seriously*. Evidence shows that the cavemen were the first to embrace their inner shine, using flakes of mica to add sparkle to their cave drawings.

I was meant to sparkle

IN 2017, AN OHIO WOMAN
HAD HER REVENGE WHEN SHE

"*glitter-bombed*"

HER FORMER BOSS'S OFFICE.
BUT DON'T GET ANY IDEAS:
SHE WAS ARRESTED FOR VANDALISM.

I GUESS SOME PEOPLE DON'T
APPRECIATE A CHIC MAKEOVER.

Glitter is my Happy Place

YOU SPARKLE

THE MOST WHEN

YOU ARE YOU

Ever dreamed of being covered in glitter?

Of *course* you have—and here's your chance! The only things you will need are:

Paintbrush or makeup brush
Clear hair gel
Cosmetic glitter

1. Use the brush to paint skin with hair gel.

2. Lightly pat glitter onto gelled skin with the same brush.

You'll be outshining the sun in minutes

Hey,

glitter artiste,

messes are for the birds! Keep a paper plate or large sheet of paper under your project. When you're done crafting, use a funnel to return the excess glitter to its container.

During the nineteenth century, glitter
was made from powdered or ground glass
known as diamantine. As you might imagine,
flying pieces of glass aren't the best idea.

IF ONLY PROTECTIVE EYEWEAR HAD
BEEN IN SEASON. THANKFULLY, WE HAVE
MANY *SAFE* OPTIONS TO CHOOSE
FROM NOWADAYS!

Add a little sparkle to your step—or dance!—with glitter tights.

All you need is:

Pair of plain tights
Spray adhesive
Glitter

let's see that

Next:

1. Lay the tights flat and spray with adhesive.

2. Sprinkle your glitter onto the tights.

3. Let dry, then flip tights over onto the other side and repeat.

twinkling twirl!

LEAVE A LITTLE SPARKLE

WHEREVER YOU WANDER

Lead a life that glitters

"You're not fully dressed until you sparkle"

That's too
much glitter

—SAID NO ONE EVER

Want next-
level nails
worthy of
your shining
personality?

All you need is:

Sheet of paper
Solvent-resistant glitter
Clear nail lacquer

Next:

1. Use paper to funnel glitter into lacquer.

2. Mix well, then apply.

Presto!
A magical manicure!

Unless the label says "biodegradable," glitter is one thing you *can't* toss in the recycling bin. Those little plastic particles won't be kind to our planet! So when you've got glitter garbage, empty it in a plastic bag and tie the bag shut before throwing it in the trash.

Look out, Dorothy:

You *don't* need

to leave home

for these

Oz-worthy

glittery pumps.

All you'll need is:

Paintbrush
Mod Podge
Plain heels
Glitter
Hair spray

Then:

1. Use paintbrush to apply generous coat of Mod Podge to heels.

2. Douse 'em in glitter! Make sure to get every angle.

3. Let dry, then mist lightly with hair spray.

Now you're ready to see the Wizard!

Carpet getting a little too shimmery?

Run a vacuum to nab any loose
glitter, then dab the area with
a wet paper towel to get
those deeper particles.

Stubborn sparkles be gone!

If glitter

can't help

you, then

nothing can.

get your sparkle on

FRIENDS WILL
BE DESPERATE
FOR THE DEETS
ON HOW TO
MAKE THIS
SELFIE-WORTHY
SPARKLING
PHONE CASE.

1. Mix glitter with Mod Podge in a bowl.

2. Use a foam brush to paint the mixture onto a plain phone case.

3. Let dry, then get snapping!

I see glamorous new pics in your future...

What could
be more luxurious
than wearing
gold?

Eating it!

From gold-flecked sushi to gilded chocolate cake, restaurants around the world offer dishes with a special ingredient: *glittering gold flakes!*

Bet we know where you're dining for your next birthday!

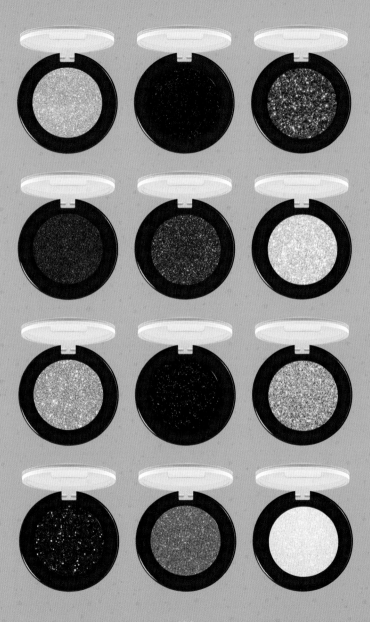

Dinner with friends, night at the movies, trip to the local market—whatever the occasion, you'll turn heads faster than royalty with this easy DIY pressed-glitter eyeshadow:

1. Apply standard eyeshadow with makeup brush.

2. Use the same brush to dab cosmetic glitter onto eyeshadow, then press with your fingertip to ensure the glitter fully sticks.

3. Make your shimmer stand out even more with a flirty cat-eye.

Life is always better with a closet full of glitter.

TALK ABOUT
BAMBOOZLED BASS:
GLITTER IS OFTEN USED
ON FISH LURES
TO MIMIC IRIDESCENT
SCALES OF REAL
FISH!

Got a mane full of glitter and somewhere to be?

Deep breaths,
we've got you covered:

1. Saturate the sparkly areas with conditioner.

2. Run a fine-toothed comb through these areas.

3. Rinse thoroughly, then wash your hair normally.

You've got this!

Sparkle with all your heart

WHO KNEW A
BUG
COULD BE
GLAMOROUS?!

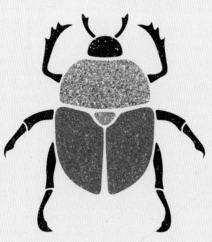

The elytra (hard outer wings) of beetles, such as
those of the Egyptian scarab, reflect dazzling
metallic greens and violets, just like gems.

WHETHER YOU'RE A MODERN
PICASSO OR MORE OF A
STICK-FIGURE SPECIALIST,
THERE'S A WAY TO UNLEASH YOUR
INNER GLITTER ARTIST:

with easy
abstract canvas art!

Ta-da!

FRIENDS WILL INSIST THAT IT'S
STORE-BOUGHT.

What you'll need:

Masking tape
Plain art canvas
Paintbrush
Mod Podge
Glitter

Next:

1. Tape off canvas to create the pattern you want to make.

2. Paint over canvas with Mod Podge.

3. Pour on your glitter.

4. Let dry, then tap the canvas over a piece of paper to shed any excess glitter.

5. Carefully peel off tape.

GLITTER IS ALWAYS AN OPTION

may your day sparkle

Favorite ensemble shedding its shimmer?

Spray it gently with hair spray to contain its shine!

Too much spray will dull the glitter,

though, so keep it modest.

Who DOESN'T *Love* glitter?

Surprisingly, there are a few people, which is why Australian native Mathew Carpenter started

Ship Your Enemies Glitter.

With the click of a button,
you could send an anonymous card
packed with glitter
to someone in need of a little "bedazzling."

KNIGHTS IN SHINING ARMOR *do* EXIST!

Clothing and artifacts

embellished with gold

have been found in the tombs of Scythian
nomadic horsemen. These fashion-forward
warriors were glistening through the landscapes
of Europe and Asia as early as 800 B.C.

YOU
ARE
a big
ball of
AWESOME
dipped in
glitter

life won't sparkle unless you do

It's sweet,
it's sparkly—
it's homemade glitter!

With a few simple ingredients,
you can make a tasty, nontoxic glitter
that you *know* will be safe around
curious little hands—or paws:

Granulated white sugar
Food coloring
Plastic sandwich bag

Now...

1. Add sugar and food coloring to sandwich bag, close, and shake well.

2. Open bag and set in bright area to dry.

Once dry, your sugary accessory is ready to jazz up any confection— or sample directly!

People will be sending their compliments to the chef!

Ready to change up those sparkly nails?

Moisten a cotton ball with acetone and hold it on the nail for a few minutes.

You can
also use a rubber
band or tinfoil to
secure the cotton
ball in place.

The acetone
will melt away the
polish sticking the glitter
to the nail, making
removal a whole
lot easier.

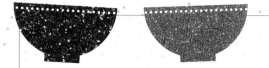

Boring ol' *coffee table* in need of a little zing?

Create a unique glitter catch-all
with these easy-to-find items:

Mod Podge
Glitter
Balloon
Paintbrush

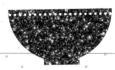

Then...

1. Mix together Mod Podge and glitter.

2. Blow up the balloon and use paintbrush to thickly coat one half with glitter mixture.

3. Let sit until Mod Podge is completely dry, then one...two...three...pop the balloon!

BAM!

A centerpiece that kicks things up a notch

YOU CAN'T HANDLE ALL THIS SPARKLE

This book belongs to:

my sparkle
cannot be
contained

YOU KNOW **WHAT** IT'S MADE OF, BUT DO YOU KNOW **HOW** IT'S MADE?

Color is applied to a sheet of plastic polymer that is glued to a sheet of reflective material like aluminum.

You might think that with three layers, the sheet must be pretty thick, but it's actually thinner than a standard piece of paper!

This layered sheet is then pulled over and under the spinning cylinders of a rotary crusher while a serrated cylinder rolls across it, cutting it into identical pieces of shimmer.

Sure, it's not a glamorous process, but hey—even pearls come from dirt.

Give the
gift of glitter
this season
with glitter
ornaments!

All you need is:

Glass bulb ornaments
Floor finish
Piece of paper
Fine glitter

Now...

1. Remove metal ornament caps (for use later) and pour a tablespoon of floor finish into each bulb.

2. Use paper to funnel glitter into bulbs, then swirl the bulbs around to coat the inside of the ornament with the glitter mixture.

3. Pour out excess mixture and let bulbs dry for 10 minutes before replacing metal caps. Tie off each ornament with a sparkly bow and share the shimmer with friends and family this year.

Ancient Egyptians, a.k.a. *Glamour Supreme*, used ground green malachite in their cosmetics to give it a radiant shimmer.

No wonder we still draw inspiration from them *thousands* of years later.

CARPE
the
SPARKLE
out of this
DIEM

ANYTHING'S POSSIBLE *with a* **LITTLE GLITTER**

start each
day with a grateful heart
&
a handful of glitter

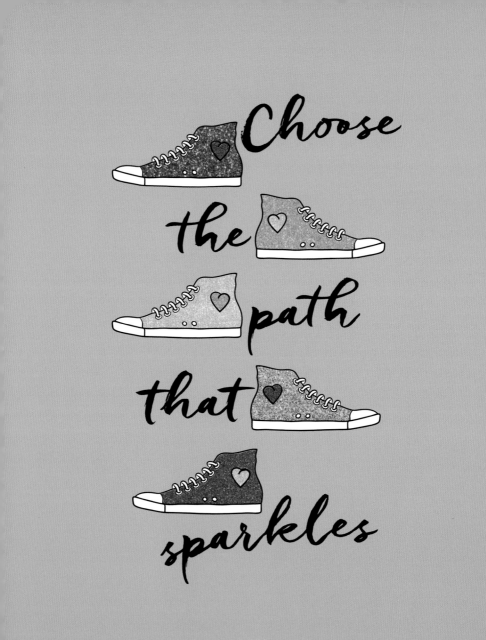

Choose the path that sparkles

Image Credits

page 1: © Getty Images/Dimitris66
page 12: © Getty Images/surachetkhamsuk
page 13: © Getty Images/scyther5
pages 14–15: © 123RF/Anastasiia Ivanskaia
page 16: © 123RF/POLINA ELYUTINA ELYITINA
page 17: © 123RF/monbibi
pages 18–19: © Shutterstock/oatawa
pages 20–21: © Getty Images/maximmmmum
page 23: © Getty Images/Tarzhanova
page 24: © Shutterstock/Slanapotam
page 25: © Getty Images/ElizaLIV
pages 26–27: © Getty Images/LysenkoAlexander, surachetkhamsuk
pages 28–29: © Getty Images/worldofvector, ChiccoDodiFC; 123RF/Anastasiia Ivanskaia
pages 30–31: © Getty Images/Photoplotnikov, surachetkhamsuk, ChiccoDodiFC
page 32: © Getty Images/hynci
page 33: © Getty Images/cutelittlethings, surachetkhamsuk
pages 34–35: © Shutterstock/Mila_1989
page 36: © Getty Images/layritten
page 37: © Getty Images/Nina_Piankova
pages 38–39: © Getty Images/wacomka
pages 40–41: © Getty Images/sofiaworld, RobinOlimb
pages 42–43: © Getty Images/Cheremuha, surachetkhamsuk; 123RF/Anastasiia Ivanskaia
pages 44–45: © Getty Images/lamika
page 46: © Getty Images/By Pirina; 123RF/Anastasiia Ivanskaia
page 47: © Getty Images/mawielobob; 123RF/Anastasiia Ivanskaia
page 48: © Getty Images/Luda311
page 49: © Getty Images/Kumer
page 50: © 123RF/katisa
page 51: © Getty Images/Mila_1989
page 52: © Getty Images/Mila_1989
page 53: © Getty Images/Barrirret
pages 54–55: © Getty Images/LenkaSerbina; 123RF/Anastasiia Ivanskaia
page 56: © Getty Images/maximmmmum
page 57: © Getty Images/golubovy
page 58: © 123RF/katisa
page 59: © 123RF/nezabudkina; Getty Images/surachetkhamsuk
pages 60–61: © Getty Images/SlothAstronaut; 123RF/Anastasiia Ivanskaia
page 62: © 123RF/CatLane

The following pages can be removed and used as decorations. Intensify their sparkle— and make them your very own—with a little glue and your favorite color glitter!

LIVE LOVE SPARKLE